CONNOTARY

winner of the 2021 Frost Place Chapbook Competition

CONNOTARY

poems

Ae Hee Lee

BULL★CITY
PRESS

DURHAM, NORTH CAROLINA

Connotary
Winner of the 2021 Frost Place Chapbook Competition

Copyright ©2021 by Ae Hee Lee.

All rights reserved. No part of this book may be reproduced,
scanned, or distributed in any printed or electronic form without
permission.

Library of Congress Cataloging-in-Publication Data

Names: Lee, Ae Hee, author.
Title: Connotary : poems / Ae Hee Lee.
Description: Durham, North Carolina : Bull City Press, [2021]
Identifiers: LCCN 2021030050 | ISBN 9781949344288 (paperback)
Subjects: LCGFT: Poetry.
Classification: LCC PR9520.9.L44 C66 2021 | DDC 811/.54--dc23
LC record available at https://lccn.loc.gov/2021030050

Printed in the United States of America

Book design by Spock and Associates

Cover artwork: *Green Flash* by Stephanie Law,
©2021 by Stephanie Law

Published by BULL CITY PRESS
1217 Odyssey Drive
Durham, NC 27713
www.BullCityPress.com

CONTENTS

Words are our weakest hold on the world.
— Alberto Ríos

HYU :: IN-BETWEEN

At all sides, the trains slip away from us.
    My sister and I play Red Light, Green Light

but with eyes closed and singing instead:
    the-hi-bis-cus-sy-ria-cus-has-bloomed-a-gain!

Our mother glances at the platform clock
    and us, as we practice the art of climbing stairs

slowly, anoint each step with the shadows of scissors, wolves,
    shapeshifters we call hands. It's a quiet

and passionate affair—to dwell
    in the meanwhile, with a waiting so bright

red like the beads of jujube fruits
    our grandmother used to dry

out in the yard, so they would amass all
    the sweetness of the world in their little bodies.

She taught me nothing is wasted
    in waiting, and to be grateful for the sun,

which won't ever hurry. Years after, she's no longer with us.
      I hum: *mu-gung-hwa-kkoch-i-pieo-sseub-ni-da!*

And a train nuzzles the station,
      as it arrives, arrives, and arrives.

KIMCHI :: IN TRUJILLO

I.

My mother and her wooden cooking spoon. A pot filled with water
and an ambiguous amount of all-purpose flour
instead of rice flour. She stirs. The water turns milky. It turns
thicker, stickier—the smell of starch dissipates into the air.
It occurs to me that my mother's arm is an orbiting moon, unable to escape
the gravity of a planet much larger than itself.

II.

My mother with salt on the palm of her hand, her arm extending
toward a ray of noon. She compares the Peruvian salt to another
memory. This unfamiliar salt in front of her eyes
is a thinner crystal. She licks her fingers. It's slightly sour.
She asks me to come and have a taste, but I
have nothing to compare it with yet.

III.

My mother slicing onions, spring onions, radishes—
into whatever size she thinks would be "a pleasure to eat."
My mother's measuring tool: her intuition, her philosophy

that a fixation with perfection deters one from pouring jeong
into the food. Jeong, she teaches me, is love
that comes with time, similar to the process of fermentation,
similar to the slow dyeing of brined leaves.

IV.

My mother's concave back as she squats over the blue rim
of a plastic tub in the laundry room. The Napa cabbages inside are
as wide as my childish hips—rare in Trujillo, rare like the Korean pepper flakes
my mother has been saving by mixing them with ají panca. The translucent
plastic gloves covering her hands are smeared with bright candy red
and the green of spring onions. She tells me to go sleep first. I dream of her
hands carefully running between the cabbage leaves, even today,
half a continent away, making sure no white spot is left untouched.

EL MILAGRO :: EDGES

"This is what the sun would taste like
if stored in a fridge," Alejandra says,

as she hands me a perfectly round
slice of pineapple, chilled,
half dressed in a thin plastic bag.

She smiles, her face casting
an umbra, in which I am

a visitor.
Once I read each heart knows
its own bitterness,

and no one else
can share its joy. But we sit, our backs

mothered by this wall.
We: a brief intersection
of elbows, a small choir of helpless slurps—

our mouths flooding and the juice
dripping freely, dribbling down

7 ·

the length of our tanned fingers,
down to dot
the sand until we reach

the middle—tough
to the touch of our teeth.

I mistake it for seed, but it's not
seed. It's corazón, coeur,
a core—

what brings together
a fruit's flesh.

She eats until her hands empty,
while I don't. It's hard
and not so sweet.

HAN-SUM :: BREATH, SINGULAR

Literally, *han-sum* means the same
    strand of wind just unspooled
a little further.

◦

    I sigh, and it's as if I've blown
onto my father's brow
until it crumples—

◦

There's endlessness
in this word: an inward-
stretching universe of lungs
            and dark matter.

◦

At my sighing habit,
    my father rephrases
        an idiom, says, *at this rate*
the draft will cleave

the ground under your feet,
    make the earth flicker
out like a sparkler's afterglow.

○

I'm assured
even the smallest breath can
            ripple.

TRUJILLO :: HOMECOMING

Alejandra welcomes me back
to our first home, her arms
wide ferns, her fingers wispy
fronds curling toward
me, toward a small sun
blushing on my cheek. She puckers
her lips to greet the wind
which sings secretly, close to my ear—
Alejandra welcomes me back
and my heart stutters. I don't
remember whether to turn my face left
or right. I whisper, *it's okay,*
es normal—for there to be sorrow
in forgetting how to cross
through gaps, now filled
with gossamer veils of time.
Gwaenchanh-a, está bien—
for people to become strangers
to their own bodies, question
why absences insist
on weaving something new.
Alejandra welcomes me back,
so I go—receive her beso:

I unfurl deeper into green,
under the embrace of lush,
unfamiliar arms.

LA ESPERANZA :: POINCIANA TREE

In La Esperanza stands a barren poinciana tree.
We climb over it, scratching its callused bark
with our sandals. Breathless, our faces
are like berries, petite and round
flames. We place airy leaflets behind our ears
and chuckle. The neighbor doesn't like us
on the tree, which extends its branches
toward her eaves, and so one day,
we come back to a nest of barbed wires
scrawled on the treetop. *How sad...*
we say to no one in particular,
How pitiful, our poinciana tree...
With the belief it would rather be
hurt by us, we leave it
to play house in a different garden.

CHICAGO :: RE-ENTRY RITUAL

I've become an expert
    at packing exactly 50 lbs.
worth of breadcrumbs.
    The luggage: the head
I unload mid-flight. I leave
    a snowy trail over the Pacific.
The fish swallow my way back,
    but I know the tale
will remain. Upon landing,
    I look back; my eyes crust
with salt. I wander through
    the labyrinth of customs,
praying for safe passage
    in a mixed tongue.
What's the purpose of your visit?
    they ask. *What's the purpose of me?*
I ask and answer myself:
    to be reunited with love, waiting
at every side of a border,
    to consider a country isn't a womb
though a womb can be a country,
    to carry the migrant dust
on my limbs, the remnant
    skin cells from people
who embraced me goodbye,

to let them weigh my hems,
to die like a candle to a kiss
        at each point of entry—rename
my departures into returns.

BONGSUNG-A :: IMPATIENT BALSAM

Monsoon in Busan, garden balsams
plump with rain. My cousin and I gather them greedily,
and we arrive to her house, our arms fragrant and shining.
She crushes the flowers, whole with silky stem, and we take
turns wrapping the paste around the curve of our childish fingers.
The weight of moist petals presses against our virgin nailbeds,
stains the plates glistening orange-red. I look for meaning
in everything, and here: the belief in true love
if the color lasts until first snow.

Lake Michigan at the coda of a polar vortex. At the edge,
I can't distinguish snow from foam, but I'm sure the ice would
taste sweet with its coral glow. My cuticles flake under the gloves—
my nails thirst. I think of all the promises that have yet
to be made. I remain a stranger to many myths, but not this.

SIJO :: MEETING POINT

Wisconsin's sky this evening is a glass
               half full of storm clouds.
For a second, they are also mountains, lilac,
               haloing the rooftops of Cajamarca.
But I'm not there
               nor now.

MENDING :: SAN AGUSTÍN

It's said that by gifting
shoes to your loved ones
you risk them
leaving you.

⚬

Yet, my father
suggests I should try
on the ones in the shop
window, fully
in the knowledge
they'll spirit me away.

⚬

The shoes are tanned
leather, the color of quail.
They hold me up
like bones.

⚬

They carry me
to Michigan, along
the lake, in search of bus stops
through snow, coasting
highways, they stop
at the occasional orange
lamplight suspended
in an alien darkness.

➵◯

They collapse
gradually, steadily
at the heels.
Both of their toe tips
bruise with salt.

➵◯

Once the strings
finish fraying, they gape
like lilies, tired
from completing
a blossoming.

It's summer.
We go back to Trujillo,
where a desert's winter
begins to whistle.

❧

My mother takes us
to the cobbler
by the church of San Agustín.
She haggles, while I keep
the shoes tucked under
my arms, covering their eyes
as if they were a small animal.

❧

In the airport again,
caught in a layover. My eyes
fall upon the new soles,
stamped with a brand
I don't recognize.
The leather has been painted
over, but some scratches
remain for good.

—○—

For this, which warms
my feet, for every senseless
reason considered
enough, gratitude knots
my heart tighter.

—○—

Around me, crowded
steps land on polished floor,
sounding a mess
of colorful pearls, spinning
off into all directions.

MIDWEST :: EQUINOX

For most of my life, I slept
by the music of sand dunes
shifting yearlong. But today I
wake up, spot a snowflake
melting into the window's glass.
I think I'll never grasp the true
width of the world. Because even this
land is a trickster, bidding
the ivory humps of winter
leviathans to thaw
into strings of water, scurry
and make a sea out of a sloping garden.
I hurry outside. I witness the way
a warm whisper rouses children
of tiny green fingers.

KOREA :: THINGS TO REVIEW BEFORE LANDING

My origin story:

My mother found me as a chestnut dangling from a tree.
When I fell onto her lap, she was eating
a copper pear with one hand, paging through
a book with the other. She carried out the burr
in the hollow of her arms; the spiny cupule made her bleed,
but she didn't let go until I broke out from the shell.
Later, I sprouted needles anew, afraid
I was being nibbled away by the world.

My grandfather's name: I thought my grandfather's name was Hal-abeoji,
only to find out it was the Korean word for grandfather.
He was the one who taught me and my sister to sail
a paper kite over a frozen river, to allow my index to flirt
with its mercurial tail.

An idiom:

When I was given a norigae to hang
under my first hanbok jacket, I foresaw
a pendulous love in my life. I alternated
between laughing and sobbing. Short horns
appeared on my back. From then on, a childlike
misfortune took the shape of a blank page
and muffled my steps in every new country I called
home. I didn't want her at first, but eventually grew
fond of her, held her hand when she cried at night.

A road: The one I took to school when I lived in Jang-yu
for that one year. I studied the occasional
bush of forsythias on the side
prodding yellow against an absolute autumn sky.

MOGYOKTANG :: INSIDE

From the entrance, the steam smells of pine leaf
and boiled eggs—I sink

into one of the hot tubs, quickly become raw skin,
conditioned timidity I can't reason away, mauve heat

blush with a nervous eye on a towel, which assured me
it would conceal the soft folds of my stomach. I'm not

alone. There are others more accustomed to bareness,
close by. Today, we all wear the same teal

waters, every quivering droplet: together
we tread the tiled floor as moons

of milk fat, of dark budding nipples and creviced
thighs, of wide stony hips, of tender

skin, exfoliated from mineral sweat and grime—and I, pulse
and curve, feel lightheaded in the

warm water, or the beauty of something so ordinary
like the body. Inside this mogyoktang, I start

to believe I can hide away from eyes and words
that hunger. I lean back, drift

into a time long before shame
was something to dress for.

MADRUGADA :: SMALL HOURS

6:03 a.m. and unripe sunlight percolates through air, canopy of oak, window and yellow curtain, into my living room. It must have been a day like this:

The birth of a word.

The word an offering,
    hatching within a fertile mind.

The instance a small god
    many have beheld at least once:

        a large jellyfish with the body of an unraveling clementine, passing through—

The house billows. Luminous cells skip across the walls, and even the gray couch gleams, flecks of morning made crescent with the shadow of leaf.

NATURALIZATION :: MIGRATION

At a pottery sale,
I buy nothing, only
      consider: this

     turquoise-ribbed vase, baked
     into a gloss of rivers,
slightly slanted to the left.

So, so cheap—perhaps
a uniqueness mistaken
      for a mistake.

I'm convinced
   of its fragility,
      its ceramic pelvis.

   The space
   it would take up
in the immigration bag

   my parents passed down
to me: dark, foldable closet
      I've dragged

from country to country.
When I was younger,
        I orphaned many books;

now I just carry
this guilt,
    a longing

    for roots, a garland
of delicate hair seeping
        slowly into soil—

into vase.
        But I'm no perennial
    green. I have feet

eager to get naked,
        moved by the seasons
not here yet.

            They ask me to chase
        their undulating
animal dreams.

BOUGAINVILLEA :: PAPELILLOS

Alejandra says she doesn't believe in discovery,
only in encounters, and that she wants to introduce me
to a bougainvillea bush down the street. She leads us
past white window gates from colonial times
that look like ornate birdcages, and I don't ask out loud
whether a single dust particle has remained
in place since I left Trujillo years ago. She points, smiling,
*Look, the branches of papelillos are over there—hugging
the sky. They are the color of our mornings here, of light
shivering in fog, busy with petals that are not petals but
leaves holding invisible flowers.* We don't stand too close;
we don't interrupt the rustle of paper chalices
above our heads. We wait, under the latticed shade, stay
still to understand what it means to sway.

SIJO :: GENEALOGY

My father liked to tease with an old pun,
                saying he found me
under the *dari*, the arch
                of my mother's *dari*, her splayed legs—
I felt fortunate to be called
                the daughter of a bridge.

ACKNOWLEDGMENTS

I am grateful to the editors of the following journals, in which versions of these poems first appeared:

"Bonsung-a :: Impatient Balsam" and "Madrugada :: Small Hours" in *The Adroit Journal*

"Sijo :: Genealogy" in *The Arkansas International*

"Trujillo :: Homecoming" in *Colorado Review*

"Kimchi :: In Trujillo" (as "Memory Series of Umma Making Kimchi in Trujillo") in *Crab Orchard Review*

"Chicago :: Re-entry Ritual," "Mending :: San Agustín" (as "Mending of Shoes"), and "Korea :: Things to Review Before Landing" in *The Georgia Review*

"Mogyoktang :: Inside" (as "Inside a Mogyoktang in Chicago") in *Nimrod International Journal*

"Han-sum :: Breath, Singular" in *Small Orange Journal*

"Hyu :: In-Between" and "El Milagro :: Edges" in *Southeast Review*

I am deeply grateful to the Palm Beach Poetry Festival and the creative writing programs at the University of Notre Dame and the University of Wisconsin-Milwaukee for providing me with the space and time to write and revise. To Woodland Pattern Book Center for everything they do for Milwaukee's literary and arts community.

To Brenda Cárdenas, Ilya Kaminsky, James Vanden Bosch, Johannes Göransson, Joyelle McSweeney, Liam Callanan, L. S. Klatt, Mauricio Kilwein Guevara, Orlando Menes, and Rebecca Dunham for their encouragement and insight.

To Ross White, Noah Stetzer, and everyone at Bull City Press for the honor to work with them and the care they have shown to this chapbook.

To Tiana Clark for seeing this small, wandering manuscript and giving it a yet another place to call home.

To Alethea Tusher, Alessandra Simmons, Caleb Nelson, heidi andrea restrepo rhodes, Ina Cariño, Kattia Quintanilla, Rachael Uwada Clifford, Siwar Masannat, and Yan Hu. For their friendships and brilliance.

To my Umma, Appa, and Donseng, who journey with me still and constantly let me know they will always be there for me.

To Daniel, for listening, for his love.

ABOUT THE AUTHOR

Born in South Korea and raised in Peru, **Ae Hee Lee** is an immigrant, scholar, translator, and poet currently living in Milwaukee. She is the author of two poetry chapbooks: *Dear bear,* (Platypus Press, 2021) and *Bedtime ‖ Riverbed* (Compound Press, 2017). She holds an MFA from the University of Notre Dame, where she was awarded an Academy of American Poets Prize, and a PhD in Literature and Creative Writing from the University of Wisconsin-Milwaukee. Her poetry has been published in *The Georgia Review*, *New England Review*, *The Southern Review*, and elsewhere.

ABOUT THE FROST PLACE CHAPBOOK COMPETITION

The Frost Place is a nonprofit educational center for poetry and the arts based at Robert Frost's old homestead, which is owned by the Town of Franconia, New Hampshire. In 1976, a group of Franconia residents, led by David Schaffer and Evangeline Machlin, persuaded the Franconia town meeting to approve the purchase of the farmhouse where Robert Frost and his family lived full time from 1915 to 1920 and spent nineteen summers. A board of trustees was given responsibility for management of the house and its associated programs, which now include several conferences and seminars, readings, a museum located in the Frost farmhouse, and yearly fellowships for emerging American poets.

The Frost Place Chapbook Competition awards an annual prize to a chapbook of poems. In addition to publication of the collection by Bull City Press, the winning author receives a fellowship to The Frost Place Poetry Seminar, a cash prize, and week-long residency to live and write in The Frost Place farmhouse.

2021   Ae Hee Lee, *Connotary*
        SELECTED BY TIANA CLARK

2020   Armen Davoudian, *Swan Song*
        SELECTED BY PATRICK DONNELLY

2019   Cassandra J. Bruner, *The Wishbone Dress*
SELECTED BY EDUARDO C. CORRAL

2018   Yuki Tanaka, *Séance in Daylight*
SELECTED BY SANDRA LIM

2017   Conor Bracken, *Henry Kissinger, Mon Amour*
SELECTED BY DIANE SEUSS

2016   Tiana Clark, *Equilibrium*
SELECTED BY AFAA MICHAEL WEAVER

2015   Anders Carlson-Wee, *Dynamite*
SELECTED BY JENNIFER GROTZ

2014   Lisa Gluskin Stonestreet, *The Greenhouse*
SELECTED BY DAVID BAKER

2013   Jill Osier, *Should Our Undoing Come Down Upon Us White*
SELECTED BY PATRICK DONNELLY